Olga

Ann-Marie Moreno

Published by Ann-Marie Moreno
Publishing partner: Paragon Publishing, Rothersthorpe
First published 2025

© Ann-Marie Moreno , London

Back cover photo: Olga with her family - Sarah, Simon and Salma

The rights of Ann-Marie Moreno to be identified as the author of this work have been asserted by her in accordance with the Copyright, Designs and Patents Act of 1988.
All rights reserved; no part of this publication may be reproduced, stored in a retrieval system, or transmitted in any form or by any means, electronic, mechanical, photocopying, recording or otherwise without the prior written consent of the publisher or a licence permitting copying in the UK issued by the Copyright Licensing Agency Ltd. www. cla. co.uk

ISBN 978-1-78792-112-2

Book design, layout and production management by Into Print
www. intoprint.net
+44 (0)1604 832149

Contents

Foreword 5

The Girl From Guyana 7

A Word About My Forefathers and -Mothers 13

The Guyana I Remember 21

Daily Life In My Guyana 27

Moving On Up 33

London Here I Come 41

Becoming Mrs Qasim 48

And Then We Were Three 55

Olga Qasim: Teacher and Houseowner 61

The Rest is History…Poetry…and Peace 64

Olga, today.

FOREWORD

As I gather up my weekly shopping from the boot of my car, my next-door neighbour Olga is on the front steps of her house saying goodbye to one of her many students who come to her for home tutoring.

As the student departs, I return her – as always – smiling greeting.

"What was it today, Olga?"

"GCSE Science," she replies. It could just easily have been A Level Physics or Maths, perhaps even a bit of English Literature or, on occasions, Latin or French.

"I've got Sarah coming over shortly. She wants me to go over standard deviation with her as she needs to brush up on it for her work," she adds. (The youngest in Olga's family, Sarah, is an analyst now in her 40s).

For Olga Qasim – Armstrong that was – is a mentally agile, 87 year-old lady who continues to help put local youngsters through their paces in any one of a number of subjects.

Amazing? Certainly. But then this is an amazing woman, whose whole life has been dedicated to imparting knowledge since the days in her parents' sitting room where, as a nine-year old, she would gather the local children together during school holidays and set them about their "lessons".

More impressive still: Olga hails from Guyana, a small country on the northeast coast of South America.

There being no national university at that time, she came to the UK on her own as a 20 year-old in 1958 to continue her education and embark on her pathway into teaching. Almost seven decades later she continues in that vocation, now often tutoring the children and grandchildren of those she used to teach in a local school.

From her childhood and teenage years in Guyana, to her studies and working life in the UK, Olga has met every challenge in her life with aplomb. She has come on an impressive journey and has no plans – even at 87 – to give up tutoring. This is the story of Olga: scientist, teacher, wife (briefly), mother to three, house owner, prize-winning poet and, of course, my neighbour, friend and self-effacing local inspiration.

1
The Girl From Guyana

"Olga, Olga, where are you now? Where is that girl!" From my perch on the tree, I can hear my mother calling. I am hiding away knowing that, if seen, I will be called upon to come in and help my sister Jean with some tedious household chore.

I loved that garden: it was like our own private jungle filled with trees and bushes and vegetables and a gaggle of geese, turkeys and pigs scrubbing about in the yard. It seemed to my seven year-old self to go on for miles but no doubt if I were to go back there today, I would be disappointed to see it was not that much bigger than my own back garden in north London. However, whereas the latter backs onto a mainline railway track which at night sets the house shuddering as the heavy freight trains pass by, the house in Guyana boasted a stream feeding into a pond where my big brothers would swim around, splashing me as I shrieked in joy at the edge.

The garden was my refuge for when I had been naughty. Not that I was particularly rebellious, but I was carefree, some would say careless. On one occasion I lost my bracelet in that garden. The bracelet must have been quite precious – it may indeed have been a Christening gift – as its loss caused quite a stir. Sister Griff, who was not in fact our sister but who came to help cook, clean and do the laundry, was the one who eventually found it, hanging off a bush. She emerged from the fronds with said item in her hand, huffing and puffing and muttering "That Olga will be the death of me."

This was the garden of our house in Vreed-en-Hoop, a small town on the west bank of the Demerara River. I was not born there, nor indeed was it the first home I remember, but it is the house I recall most fondly, and which remains in the family today.

I was born Olga Armstrong on February 7, 1938 – my saint's name Anne being added sometime later as a nod to my father's Catholic upbringing. I came into the world in Georgetown, the capital city of Guyana which sits on the east side of the Demerara River. I was the fourth in line in my family after brothers Eustace and Frankie and sister Jean. To that already sizeable brood would be added in due course my younger brothers Ken and Donald Maxwell (always known affectionately as Maxie) and a surprise half-brother Eric. With six children spread over fourteen years, my mother was kept busy in the home. Sister Griff was indispensable, and my actual sister Jean took naturally to domestic chores. Not Olga Anne Armstrong, I'm afraid to say.

We came to Vreed-en-Hoop via several other townships on the west side of the river, moving house each time my father – a policeman – was transferred or promoted. My earliest memories are not of Georgetown but of Stewartville where I attended kindergarten. We lived in a house in its own grounds which had a long driveway to the gate. It probably wasn't very long but through my young eyes it seemed so. I would chase my brother Ken, just a year younger than myself, to the gate, clearly throwing to the wind any caution a three year-old might have and which resulted on one occasion in my hurtling into the gatepost and getting a nail interred in my forehead. I did say I was careless at times. That is one memory that will never go away as I still have the scar to remind me. A far nicer reminiscence is the picnics that Mum would take us on to a stream nearby after my morning at kindergarten.

Our next home was due north of Stewartville: the coastal village of Den Amstel. It seemed like a great upheaval but in fact Google maps tells me it is only 5-6 miles from Stewartville and a similar distance from Vreed-en-Hoop to which it was linked by the Demerara-Essequibo railway. At Den Amstel we lived in a house on stilts, reached by stairs at the back and with a separate outhouse for the kitchen.

The sea was close by and when my father went swimming in the morning, we would stand in the shallows playing fishermen or holding hands and waiting for the waves to come and get us.

By this time, I had graduated from kindergarten to my first proper school: Miss Jay's Prep School. This was a private church school for boys and girls, just across the road from the police station where my father worked, and where I found early inspiration for my path towards teaching as a vocation. It wasn't a big school – in my mind's eye it looked like a cottage. My mother would accompany Ken and me there each morning while the older ones walked boldly through the fields. I was envious and would have gone along with my elder siblings until the day that Jean was chased by a herd of cows. Even so, I felt quite grown-up already and couldn't fathom why there was "baby" in my kindergarten class until it was explained to me that the poor young boy suffered from what used to be known as dwarfism.

We were picked up at midday by Nanny Elsie (as in the case of Sister Griff, no relation) who would make us lunch and vainly try to keep us in check during the afternoon while Mum was busy doing housework or – more often than not – measuring, cutting and sewing fabric into clothes for her growing family.

From Den Amstel we eventually found our way to Vreed-en-Hoop where I was to live the rest of my time in Guyana. We initially had accommodation above the police station until my father was promoted to the lofty position of Superintendent of Police and was able to purchase the house that I generally consider home. After the restraints of the apartment, where we were constantly being shushed so as not disturb the police officers below, this new house seemed a palace: two stories high and with that big rambling garden, there was more than enough space for our eight-strong family.

The house in Vreed-en-Hoop.

Me, aged about 16.

By now I had reached the advanced age of eight or nine and life was becoming more interesting. After a year or two in the local St Swithen's School, my horizons widened considerably when I was enrolled in Mr Beard's primary school in Georgetown across the river. This involved something of an epic journey for me (no SUVs dropping children off two yards from the school gates in those days!). Proudly sporting my navy-blue gymslip, I had to complete a fifteen-minute walk to the ferry terminal, followed by the ferry ride across the river then another ten or fifteen minutes on foot to the school door by nine o'clock every weekday morning. It soon became apparent that completing this routine on a daily basis was a challenge so, despite my tender years, I became a weekly boarder at the house of a family friend. I adapted quite quickly to the separation from home, though I always missed Ken. On the occasions Mum would bring me a pastie or something sweet from Brown Betty's shop after she had done her shopping, I was at that age when I was embarrassed to see her outside the school yard accompanied by my youngest brother Maxie.

Being a weekly boarder meant that, as well as cutting down on tiring travelling time, I was available in the evening for additional coaching to prepare for the government's scholarship exam. For reasons I no longer recall, though, I never did sit the scholarship exam and so ended up at Georgetown's Central High School. That, however, is another chapter.

2
A Word About My Forefathers And -Mothers

AT THIS POINT I feel I should stop talking about Olga Armstrong and tell you more about the large and loving family I was lucky enough to belong to. You have already met my siblings, but my parents and grandparents provided a strong and colourful thread running through the tapestry of my childhood and teenage years.

My mother was Frances, maiden name Ward. She was the glue in the family, the one who held us together and kept the family home functioning. She had set her sights on my father from a young age, famously telling her mother "When I grow up, I will marry him," regardless of the fact he was already married. And indeed, when his first wife died, it was Frances who was there to pick up the pieces for him and fulfil her childhood dream. My father was three times her size and fifteen years her senior, but she definitely ruled the roost. When she called, we all jumped – including my father with his characteristic response "Yes babe".

Mum hailed from Guyana's East Coast and had had a Methodist upbringing, but when she married my father, the wedding took place in a Catholic church – perhaps one of the few times my father had his way. She kept up her Methodism on visits home to the East Coast, but we were raised as Catholics and all that meant in terms of attending mass and taking First Communion.

Apart from being a very adept homemaker, Mum loved classical music and in fact named me after one of her favourite singers. While she did not play an instrument herself – at least, I never saw her doing so – she came from a musical family. Her father had not one, but two pianos at home and both her brothers were keen musicians. We never missed any concert or local musical performance if it could be helped.

Her family background was a little unorthodox. Her own mother, Mathilda Whittaker, came to Guyana from Barbados. Little is known about Grandmother Mathilda's bloodline although she aways claimed a certain degree of Scottish heritage via her Whittaker grandfather who was probably a plantation owner. Certainly, the paleness of her complexion hinted at this.

Mathilda arrived in Guyana with a childless couple who – informally it would seem – had adopted her. The husband was a pastor and teacher who had given Mathilda a good educational grounding, and indeed she was a strong influence on me and my teaching aspirations as I was growing up.

With my grandfather Earl Ward, Mathilda had two children – my mother Frances and her brother Gladstone – but they were never married. Indeed, he went on to marry someone else and father several more children. It was a peculiar set-up, both households living, as they did, in close proximity. My grandmother had little to do with Earl, but my mother was close to her half-siblings, and I can remember visiting his house and eating at a long table with a whole raft of half-uncles and aunts and cousins.

These grandparents I would visit in school holidays. They lived in the village of Beterverwagting, meaning Better Expectation in Dutch and shortened generally to BV. Years before, BV had been a sugar plantation farmed by slaves. To get there we took the ferry to Georgetown then the steam train down the coast, walking from the local station to Grandmother's. I remember fondly her little cottage by the stream where – according to the stories she would tell us – mermaids swam and sang in the moonlight. I used to peer through the shutters at the moon and stars, enthralled by her tales. From this grandmother I believe I developed my love of poetry and storytelling. I continued to visit her well into my teenage years – though perhaps with a little less credence where the mermaids were concerned – and was moved when she made the journey quite a few years later to Georgetown to see me off on my voyage of adventure across the Atlantic. And she never, even by then, lost her Barbadian accent.

Grandad Earl lived on the opposite side of the village. An engineer by trade, he for some unfathomable reason owned two identical houses – the "front house" and the "back house". Not only were the houses the same but pretty much every detail down to the gardens, the big front gates, the furniture and of course the pianos.

Although I was very close to my father, Wilfred Nathaniel Amstrong, we did not get to see his family so often. My paternal grandfather, Nathaniel, hailed from Berbice further down the coast from BV. I remember once asking my Mum who "that old man coming up the stairs" was – to which she hushed me and said, "That is your Grandfather Armstrong." For some reason I have clearer memories of Dad's brothers Algernon and Cecil whose jobs as a train driver and ferry hand respectively brought them regularly to Georgetown and so closer to our side of the river.

Our paths crossed more often with Grandfather's wife Polly Anne who would come up to Georgetown to sell her produce at the market. Occasionally she came to stay with us, always dressed in her head scarf and bringing fruit.

As well as having less contact with both these grandparents, because my father was so much older than Mum, his parents were also already quite elderly and died when I was young.

After years of admiring him from afar, my mother's formal relationship with my father began at a dance. Now a widower and fifteen years her senior, he clearly adored her. The courtship was brief and blossomed into a marriage that would endure happily until Daddy died of a heart attack at the age of seventy. Mummy – or as we all called her, Sister Baby (a name that was given to her by Dad's daughter from his first marriage) – would often sit on his lap of an evening while we children arranged ourselves on the floor around them, listening to the wireless or perhaps just mulling over the day's events.

Daddy was often away on police work, particularly after his promotion to Superintendent, when he would go upcountry by boat for what seemed to me to be ages. Mummy also went away on occasions to see her mother: I loved these periods because my father was then left to do the cooking and was far more lavish with the butter and the sugar than my mother would ever have been.

As a policeman he was well known locally and had a good insight into the lives of the people in our community. A couple of times a year he and my mother would invite the neediest of the neighbourhood into our garden for a right royal feast, Mummy setting to with Sister Griff to provide them with a wonderful spread of the best of Guyanese food.

My mother was too preoccupied with bringing up six children to spare us much affection individually, but I know she loved us each in her own way. Daddy, however, was a big cuddly bear who would sit me on his lap and call me his pet name Noonie (I could do no wrong in his eyes). He eventually retired from the police force and set up a little general stores out front. I suspect this was as much to give him ample chance to chat with the neighbours and customers as it was to supplement his police pension.

My two elder brothers Eustace and Frankie followed

Daddy into the police force. Eustace married Pat with whom – following in my parents' footsteps – he had six children. On his retirement as Chief Inspector of Police, he upped sticks and moved with Pat to the United States to be closer to their children.

Frankie was always the naughty one, regularly getting into scrapes and threatening to kick me under the table if I told Mummy I had caught him speaking the local patois instead of the King's English. Despite this, he too became a policeman, being promoted to the rank of Assistant Commissioner. Like Eustace before him, he retired to the United States with his wife Yvonne.

And then there was Jean – my only sister. We were very different characters and like most sisters, we argued a lot. We had to share a bed, and I was always being told off by her for not making my side every morning. When help was needed with the cooking or housework, Olga was never to be found but Jean, taking her cue from Mummy, was a natural homemaker. What I considered tedious, she relished. It was only natural somehow that, after a brief stint as a secretary, she would stay at home, marry her sweetheart Eddie and provide a home for her three sons. Jean – at eighty-nine, two years my senior – is still in Guyana today.

My two younger brothers – Ken and Maxie – were likewise to leave Guyana before long, Ken to the UK and Maxie to Canada via a stint as an engineer in the Royal Air Force at Brize Norton in Oxfordshire and then Malta.

My parents Wilfrid and Frances.

Adding to this already sizeable brood – though not a permanent resident Chez Armstrong – was Eric, our half-brother. Eric lived most of his time in Georgetown just round the corner from the Central High School. His mother was, I believe, of Portuguese extraction. He was very close in age to Frankie, begging the question as to *what* exactly my father got up to on his stints of work away from home. While I vaguely remember my father once packing his bags to leave, I do not know if it related specifically to Eric's existence, but Dad never actually moved out. My mother's love for our father must have been sorely stretched at some point, but Eric was always a regular and welcome visitor to our house.

3
The Guyana I Remember

I LEFT GUYANA many decades ago to come to study in the UK and although I did visit several times later, I am certain I would find my home country very much transformed today.

I grew up in what was at the time British Guiana – since 1831 a colony of the country in which I was later to settle, and which had been under British control for several decades before that. Guyana means "land of many waters", and indeed its geography and topology are very much defined by its rivers and coastline. It is the third smallest and second least populated country in South America, and because of its colonial past, is the only one where English is an official language.

It is sandwiched between Venezuela to the north and Suriname to east, both of whom for decades have laid claim to some of Guyana's territory along disputed and often inaccessible borders. To the south lies Brazil's Roraima state. Like its southern neighbour, Guyana boasts vast areas of rainforest, but unlike Brazil's, most of Guyana's is largely unspoiled – as yet.

The majority of the country's population of around 830,000 is concentrated along the coastal plain. As well as the rain forest, there are belts of savannah, lowland

and sprawling white sands containing minerals such as bauxite and silica. British colonists prised the country away from the Dutch – who at the time had greater issues to concern them at home in Europe – in the late 18th century and put the country's fertile plains to producing more sugar and other plantation crops.

Originally worked by African slaves, as emancipation gained traction in the mid-1880s the plantation workforce was gradually replaced with thousands of indentured workers brought in from the Indian sub-continent. These influxes of people from Europe, Africa and Asia have created a rich melting-pot of ethnicities, cultures and languages. Guyana's population today is some 40% Indian, 30% African, 20% mixed race and 10% indigenous peoples. The official language may still be English but Guyanese creole is spoken by the majority.

However, with the UK colonists in the driving seat for some 150 years, the Guyana I grew up in was heavily influenced by all things British (with the exception, perhaps, of the food). The education I received was based very much on the British curriculum of the time, and government structures mirrored the UK system of governance. To me it seemed quite normal and acceptable.

But rumblings of independence were getting louder as I made my preparations to leave for the country of our colonial masters. Just a few years after I reached these shores, British Guiana was no more. The independent Guyana was born in 1966, becoming the Co-operative

Republic of Guyana in 1970. Independence Day is celebrated each year on May 26.

The political, social and industrial landscape underwent tremendous changes during these years. Authoritarian Prime Minister Linden Forbes Burnham embarked on nationalising industries and expelling multinational companies such as Alcan and Reynolds. Politics became much more divided along ethnic lines, and education broke away from the British system. Schools were nationalised and many new ones built in rural areas, while A levels were abolished. The reforms did, however, lead to Guyana at long last establishing a university of its own.

Today the president is the Head of State and government rests in the National Assembly. From a military viewpoint, the army is dependent on its links with the US and Brazilian armed forces – and both these and indeed the British army have been called upon on occasions to ward off Venezuelan designs on Guyanese territory.

As colonial rule ended and successive governments grappled with modernising what was essentially a plantation-based economy dependent on agricultural and some mineral export earnings, Guyana gradually transformed itself and has taken its place on the world stage. This process was accelerated by the discovery in around 2020 of vast reserves of crude oil off the Atlantic coast, boosting GDP and earning the country the tag of "Qatar of South America".

I am not sure what my country will do with this newfound wealth but hope and pray it will be to the benefit of all my fellow Guyanese, and not at the expense of its beautiful and biodiverse flora and fauna.

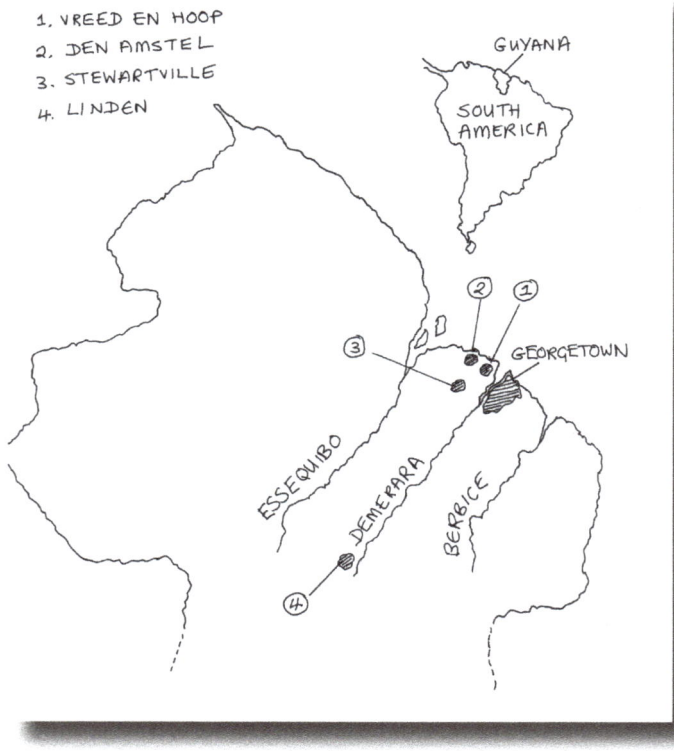

4
Daily Life in My Guyana

OF COURSE THAT was the bigger picture. My daily routines and pastimes were a microcosm within it. Life revolved mainly around Vreed-en-Hoop and Georgetown, with occasional forays slightly further afield. School, family, food and friendships were the mainstays of my childhood and adolescence, and today, over sixty years on, I still feel a warm glow of nostalgia when I hark back to those days. At family gatherings my children – whose first-hand knowledge of Guyana is relatively scant – beg me to make rotis, or pepper pot or cook-up rice, and as I stand at the stove the aroma of the spices can send my mind drifting back to our old Vreed-en-Hoop kitchen with my mother standing over the charcoal stove cooking for her hungry family.

Although my grandmother, I recall, used to cook on a coal fire in the kitchen, we eventually graduated from the charcoal stove to – luxury of luxuries – a calor gas cooker which made Mum's life easier. At least I guess so: the closest I got to it was to sneak the odd taste while she wasn't looking.

Just like the ethnic make-up of its people, Guyanese food derives from a veritable mixture of cuisines, with strong Indian, Chinese and local influences and ingredients. Of course, most of what we ate we reared or produced, or we bought in the local markets. Breakfast usually consisted of home-made bread and butter or bakes – similar to American biscuits – washed down with a glass of milk. Eggs too, but only for the boys if the hens were having a lazy laying day.

Lunch was often home-made patties (similar to pasties), stuffed rotis, or rice and lentils with vegetables with exotic-sounding names. Some of these in recent years have found their way into the aisles of British supermarkets: plantain; callaloo (spinach-like but with thicker leaves); okra (or okro as we called it); bolangers (our name for aubergine); root vegetables like eddoes, dashheen or sweet potatoes; yams and cassava or yucca. Most we grew in the garden, but proper "English potatoes" had to be bought in the market.

We also had plenty of fruit which Mummy would use to flavour drinking water, and if the gardener had been and climbed up, fresh coconut milk from our tall, spindly palm trees.

Dinner was at 6 o'clock on the dot – by which time my father would usually be home from work and we would all sit round the big table enjoying meals such as metemgee – a delicious vegetable broth with dumplings and coconut milk – or salt fish with fried plantains and rice.

My personal favourite was pepper pot – a spicy, warming stew of meat and peppers with cassareep (caramelised cassava root) – giving it a slightly sweet-

and-sour flavour. Lamb or chicken curry were staples too as well as noodles, black beans and rice. Sunday lunch was often the graphically-named cow-heel soup with dumplings.

The milkman came daily and would measure out the milk into jugs which we kept in an old-fashioned ice box. There was a local butcher although Mummy liked to make a weekly trip to the market in Georgetown. The fishman came once a week but we always had fish *with* scales: fish with no scales – bottom feeders and the like – were cheaper and not for a middle-class family like ours!

There were dishes that harked back to the days of the African plantation slaves: cook-up rice that we often ate at New Year to use up left-over meat, peas and vegetables; or conkie (pronounced kankee) which was a dessert of cornmeal, pumpkin, coconut, sugar and spices cooked in a banana leaf. Another sweet dish I recall – but which was probably more related to its distant British cousin – was black cake which we ate at Christmas, a rich moist, dark cake containing rum-soaked dried fruits and molasses.

Alcohol was not regularly consumed at home although my father would have the odd beer, and I can distinctly recall being chastised at my sister's engagement party for trying to sneak a sip or three of champagne!

When we were not at school, life revolved around our garden and the few streets that made up Vreed-en-Hoop, with occasional sorties to visit family or friends. Sunday mornings for some time were taken up by attendance at Catholic mass followed by Sunday school where we were taught the catechism and prepared for our First Communion. The afternoons would often see us walking along the sea wall with our parents. "Now you children, you see you don't get caught by the tide. You come back here – now!" Mummy would call as we ran free. The sea wall was dotted with turrets, and we loved – if the tide was out – to clamber round on the rocks, which led to more than a few tumbles by yours truly. Sometimes we would take the ferry across to Georgetown and visit the market and the pretty central square with its clocktower.

With my brothers we explored the area around Vreed-en-Hoop, myself perched precariously on the back of Jean's bicycle until I was old enough to have one of my own. We would go down to the creek where the boys used to swim but Jean and I just dabbled in the shallows for most of the time.

Back at the house I liked nothing more than to head off to a secluded area we called the "hip gallery" and read or write poetry or complete my homework for the following day. My younger brother Maxie often followed me round and sat next to me learning verses of Shakespeare off by heart even at his tender years.

When school holidays came around, I was often to be found practising my teaching skills on the children of our neighbourhood. "Now sit down, children and hush. This morning, we are going to do our multiplication," and I would set the uncomplaining youngsters to chant their times tables parrot-fashion while I paraded round like a Miss Jean Brodie-in-the-making.

I sometimes used to visit my Grandma Ward down the coast in BV, or my friend who lived upriver near Linden. To get there was a bit of an adventure because I had to travel by boat as they lived on an island in the river close to a bauxite processing plant.

On a few occasions I went away with the Brownies, usually by train to stay in what appeared to be a school hall on the coast. Once, on the way back, the train was derailed when a meandering cow chose suddenly to cross the track. I do not recall the fate of said animal, but the driver was sadly killed. That trip was an adventure and one I care not to repeat! Luckily, we were in the rear of the train so came off unscathed, though the fact that a group of young girls was travelling unaccompanied did cause a local sensation for a while, our Brown Owl for some unknown reason having not come with us.

The original Central High School building on Smyth Street, Georgetown, where I spent several happy years (above), and then as it was on my last visit there (below).

5
Moving On Up

GEORGETOWN CENTRAL HIGH was to become the focal point of my life for the next several years. This institution was founded in 1927, the creation of one Joseph Clement Luck – or JC as he became known. JC had gained a Bachelor of Arts Degree from London but tried his hand at many things including farming before deciding to establish a school of his own.

At that time, British Guiana was reasonably well endowed with primary schools, the churches having taken the lead on basic educational provision. Secondary schools were few and far between, however. The Guyanese government had created a number of selective and largely denominational grammar schools in Georgetown including, for boys, the Queens College and Stanislaus College, as well as two girls-only convent schools. But Central High School, still located at its original site in Smyth Street, was where I was destined to go.

This school began life with just thirty-five pupils, many of whom were drafted in to help with the construction project in return for a reduction in tuition fees. JC Luck's own children Rudy and Stella became pupils in due course and the school eventually evolved into the country's biggest private educational establishment. Much later, his youngest daughter Jane was in the same form as me, and we quickly became firm friends.

The school continued to exist long after I exited its doors, merging in 2019 with St Mary's School to become the New Central High School. The old building was renovated and is now home to the administrative division of the Ministry of Education.

I was lucky in that my parents could afford to pay for our education right up to and through our secondary school years – hardly a mean feat given that there were six of us! There was a number of scholarships on offer but as I mentioned earlier – and for reasons I appear to have blanked out – I did not sit the scholarship exam.

By the time I arrived there, in my black tunic and school tie, my eldest brother Eustace had already left to start work. Frankie was still a pupil, as was Jean, a few years above me.

At Georgetown Central High we followed a very British curriculum which would lead to my taking O Level exams under the Cambridge Senior Certificate followed, by those who stayed on, the London University Board Advanced Level exams. Latin and Maths were my favourite subjects but sadly the latter was not offered at Advanced Level, neither was Science. I opted for Latin, History and English and after two years' further study was successful in obtaining my Advanced Certificate.

In addition to working towards the much-coveted Advanced Levels exams – which would virtually guarantee entry into the Civil Service – we students were encouraged to take on extra-curricular activities. The school offered shorthand and typing courses as well as Adult Education programmes. While still at Georgetown Central, Jean completed a Pitman's course in shorthand and typing, which she then took to teacher level via evening classes at Carnegie School. Although she worked for a few years as a secretary at the Rice Marketing Board, once she married Eddie, she readily reprised the role of homemaker that she had loved so much when we were younger.

Of course, sport was important – soccer, cricket and table tennis in particular – and the school boasted a playing field alongside the building, but it was my brothers who availed themselves more of these activities while I concentrated on the academic ones.

I can still remember now my journey to Central High from home every day: the walk to the ferry terminal, then the 10-15 minute scurry through town to the school, glancing at the clocktower in the main square to make sure I was not going to be late. Lunch would be taken nearby at my half-brother Eric's mother's house, then at the end of the school day I would make the same journey back, crossing the Demerara River on the ferry once more.

When I was not at school or doing prep at home, my modest social life revolved around our family circle and a small group of girlfriends with whom I would get togged out at the weekend for shopping or cinema trips to Georgetown. If there were any boyfriends on the scene, it was all very innocent and above board, with male admirers being invited over to have tea with the family. Occasionally, though, there might be a dance where we could flaunt and flirt a little more with the opposite sex.

I eventually graduated from Central High School and followed that well-worn path into the Civil Service with a job at the City Hall in Georgetown. After a stint working there, I moved to an office job closer to home in Vreed-en-Hoop, but clearly neither post gripped me as I cannot remember what my working day entailed: I sense maybe a lot of looking out of the window and daydreaming about my future.

Georgetown City Hall where I was briefly to work after leaving high school.

Certainly, during those couple of years I was working, my plans for furthering my education started to crystallize. Staying in Guyana was not an option and while many of my friends set their sights on a university career in the United States, I was looking further afield to the United Kingdom. I had no concept of what life in the USA would be like, but after following the British curriculum for many years and despite the distance, crossing the Atlantic seemed, to my 20 year-old mind, a more natural route. In British Guiana, our everyday lives – from schooling to the Union Jack flying above Government House to my holidays with the Brownies – were dominated by the British way of life.

For Mum and Dad, though, the United Kingdom seemed a whole universe away. "Why don't you go to the United States? That's where your pals are going. You would be able to come home more often," said Dad, desperate for his younger daughter to stay closer to home.

Mum's thoughts were not so much on where but *what* I would study. Despite my A Levels in the Humanities, she dearly hoped that in daughter Olga she had a doctor in the making and had her sights set on the best medical schools the USA could offer.

"But Mum, I studied the British system. I understand A Levels and England has some excellent universities," I insisted. Also, I didn't like what was happening in the USA in terms of racial segregation, and felt Guyana's colonial links to the UK would stand me in better stead there than north of the Rio Grande.

However, under pressure from my mother, I duly sent off an application to Howard University in Washington. This institution had a fine reputation and a tradition of providing quality education for black students, in particular. At the same time, I quietly started to investigate more what I would need to study in the UK. I had few savings and so would still have to depend quite heavily on my parents for financial support, although as a Citizen of the United Kingdom and Colonies I would qualify for a student grant once I made it to university in the UK. However, that was not going to be quite straightforward given that my A Levels were in Latin, History and English. Despite Mum's ambitions for me to study Medicine and become a doctor, I harboured ambitions of becoming a Science teacher – though I said little about this to my mother. Either way, I would need to arm myself with some science-based A levels before I even applied to university.

My plans were sidetracked temporarily by a reply from Howard University saying I had been accepted to study Medicine there! My mother, obviously, was over the moon so it took all my powers of persuasion to convince her that what I most wanted was to study in the UK. Eventually she relented and my preparations continued.

I aimed to travel to London and spend a year or two acquiring the requisite science A levels before embarking on my university degree course. No-one from my family had ever undertaken such an adventure: my parents and myself alike anticipated my forthcoming departure with a mixture of excitement and apprehension. Here I was, a 20 year-old Olga who had never ventured outside Guyana, indeed rarely much beyond the fringes of Georgetown, about to cross the ocean to a new life in England.

The occasion was marked by a leaving party attended by many friends and family, with one or two male admirers making it into the group photo. Mum made my favourite meat patties, roti and curry, chow mein and pineapple tarts, and we had a great time, eating and dancing to the latest rock and roll hits before the time came for me to depart.

My send-off party. Myself, centre, wearing the obligatory hat; my mother third from right, and an assembly of siblings, nieces and admirers. My father couldn't face the emotion of a farewell at the airport.

Most of the party-goers accompanied me to the airport where I was to commence my lengthy journey to London. My father though, to whom I was particularly close, declined to come and see his daughter off. Big softie that he was, he could not have handled the emotion of the moment. He stood at the doorstep to wave me off, both of us holding back the tears as best we could.

And so began another stage of my life: little did I think at the time that from then I would only return to my homeland for brief and sporadic holidays. But I was young, excited and full of my own self-importance – and the world was suddenly my oyster.

6
London Here I Come

So, there I was, passport in hand, at Georgetown's little airport. Still known at that time as the Atkinson Aerodrome, it had begun life during the Second World War as a US airfield. No-one in my family had, to my knowledge, flown before so the level of excitement was all the more heightened. Atkinson at that time had flights to various destinations in the Caribbean and, with multiple stops en route, to the United States. However, there were no flights to the UK: my route was going to be somewhat convoluted and would take considerably longer than the direct flights operating today.

To wave me off as I boarded the flight for the short hop to Trinidad was a large group comprising my mother, my maternal grandmother, my siblings and a group of friends and would-be boyfriends. The farewell photo shows me looking very prim in a pale dress Mum had no doubt run up for the occasion, a handbag and of course the obligatory hat.

Trinidad was the first of several places we visited as we island-hopped in small turbo-prop planes via Barbados, Martinique and on to Guadeloupe. I have memories of descending over turquoise blue seas and landing on airstrips surrounded by lush green vegetation. At

Barbados I was met briefly by someone who knew my grandmother Mathilda who just came along to say hello and wish me *Bon Voyage*.

At Guadeloupe I transferred to a ship which would take me to Puerto Rico. I was beginning to realise just how small the world of Olga Amstrong had been up until that point. Guyana is smaller than England and my knowledge of even my own little country was limited to a few towns and villages in and around Georgetown.

The port at Puerto Rico seemed enormous and the ship bearing both passengers and cargo to Europe gigantic. By this time, I had teamed up with a girl of a similar age to myself so felt slightly less alone in that big wide world. She was not going to the UK to study though: rather she was heading for an arranged marriage to someone she had never met! I couldn't even fathom how that would feel, but we kept each other company, nevertheless. We boarded the ship bound for Vigo in northwest Spain. I remember little of the transatlantic voyage other than that, as mere mid-class passengers, we would sneak up to the top deck whenever we could to watch the ocean drift by.

The crossing from Puerto Rico to Europe took two weeks. At Vigo we boarded another vessel for the voyage to Portsmouth. By now Guyana was feeling very, very distant. And then, finally, the British shoreline was there on the horizon. As we disembarked, I was somewhat relieved not to be left to my own devices. I was met on the wharf by a representative of the British Council who accompanied me and some fellow students on the rail journey to London. It was autumn time, September I believe, and the sun was shining. "So," I mused "the stories about it always raining in England are not true."

I looked out of the carriage window as the train made its way to the capital, drinking in the English countryside, fields and forest. Yes, we had greenery aplenty at home, but this was different. I was entranced. The green changed into greyness as we pulled into Paddington Station. I had finally arrived in London! There I was met by one Aunt Vida, not an actual aunt but a close family friend with whom I was to spend my initiation into British life, away from the home comforts I had taken for granted and was to miss sorely during those early months.

I have to say Aunt Vida, despite taking me in, was not very nice to me – but I guess I had a lot to learn. She lived upstairs in a block of flats not far from Paddington. Vida told me from the outset "Well young lady, don't think we have servants here; you will need to learn to cook and wash and look after yourself. If you don't cook, you won't eat!"

To be honest, at the age of twenty, I had no idea how to fend for myself. We had always had help at home with cooking and washing and, unlike my sister Jean, I had never had any inclination to get involved in domestic affairs.

"Young lady, are you stupid or what? Did that mother of yours teach you nothing back home?" Aunt Vida shouted at me after my abortive attempt to boil myself an egg, not in a saucepan but in the stove-top kettle. This cardinal sin was then made all the worse by the fact that I clearly got distracted by something far more interesting then completely forgot about it until the kettle boiled dry...

I stuck it out at Aunt Vida's, as it was within walking distance of Paddington Technical College where I had enrolled to study – somewhat ambitiously – four A levels in Botany, Zoology, Physics and Chemistry.

I wrote home enthusiastically about my new college life. I lapped up the new subjects, relished the new educational challenge and getting to know London, and gradually the longing for home evolved into momentary pangs of homesickness. I began to make some new friends too. My correspondence about my home life was less enthusiastic. Things had not improved at Aunt Vida's, so after several epistles to Guyana complaining about how miserable I was there, Mum found me new lodgings with the daughter of our old Sister Griff. Although this involved a bus journey to college, I didn't mind. I would sit atop the red double-deckers absorbing the sights and sound of the capital city, so different, bigger and brasher than our sedate little Georgetown.

Things went better at my new digs – for a while at least. There was just Sister Griff's daughter, her little girl and myself for most of the time. We got on well and I enjoyed looking after the little one when her mum was busy.

Her husband wasn't around much, I guess because of his work, but at some point, he seemed to be at home a lot more and was paying his new young lodger far more attention than I felt comfortable with. I took to avoiding him and his lewd looks, but to no avail. When the looks turned to actual attempts to touch or grab me – inappropriately as they say these days – I had had enough. I confronted his wife, but she simply became angry with me and suggested I was making it up!

My mother's response was immediate: "Olga, you get yourself out of that house as soon as you can and just pray that awful man has not tried it on with that poor little girl there."

This time I had to find new digs myself but was delighted when my college friend Barbara Joseph asked me to move in with her. Barbara was a few years older than me and studying architecture. I told her of my predicament with the wandering-hands husband, and she said "Look no further. You will be safe with me." It didn't take much to persuade me to accept; moreover, her flat had the added bonus of being back closer to the college in Paddington.

We shared happy times in that flat for a couple of years. Barbara hailed from Trinidad and came from a humbler background than mine, but she was bright and committed and had won a scholarship to study. For a time, she had a boyfriend but that fizzled out and he went back to Trinidad, so for much of the time it was just us two girls. She was a real friend to me. Barbara never married but had a successful career, becoming Chief Architect at one of London's boroughs.

London was now my second home. I loved the hustle and bustle, the big red buses, the parks, the tall (mostly) elegant buildings. I missed my father enormously and I certainly missed my mother's home cooking but still, I remember writing home to my parents: "I think I will live here forever."

Occasionally, though, I could be made to feel an outsider. While nothing like the racial divisions of the USA, 1960's England was still coming to terms with its colonial past, and not all Brits were totally welcoming and friendly to people of different colour. I recall being the butt of wolf whistles and called nig-nog by a bunch of teddy boys in the street. This type of taunt I was usually able to ignore or laugh off, but I felt much more of a second-class citizen when on more than one occasion I was stopped by a policeman and asked to open my handbag for no reason whatsoever other than the colour of my skin.

I had come from a country with a melting pot of ethnicities where, if there was a degree of social hierarchy depending on your skin colour, it did not flow through to my family and personal life. The owner of my school and his deputy head were of Chinese origin, and his daughter was one of my closest friends. My father came from the East Coast where the demographics were heavily African, and this showed in Dad's accent. One time when he was sent to the northwest interior of the country to work, he brought home with him a young aboriginal girl who was being mistreated, and she lived with us as a member of the family, sharing a room with my sister and me.

Fortunately, any racist comments in London were few and far between. Nevertheless, my mother's words "You need to use your brain to get on in this world, Olga, as you don't have the right colour skin," would come back to me then, making me all the more determined to further my education and get a degree.

7
Becoming Mrs Qasim

IT WAS DURING my time with Barbara that I met my first real boyfriend. Sitting in the tiered seats of the A level lecture theatre, my eyes one day caught those of a male student several seats along from me. I had seen him before as he seemed to be doing very similar subjects to mine. That morning as we filed out, he caught up with me and commented "I am really enjoying these lessons. The teacher is excellent, don't you think? He makes everything clear." I agreed and was about to move on when he continued: "My name is Mohammed. I think we are doing the same courses. I was wondering if you would like to have a coffee with me."

He had a nice friendly smile, olive skin and dark eyes, and I couldn't refuse. In the college canteen he told me he too was studying the sciences and hoping to go on to university. Mohammed Qasim was about a year younger than me, came from a well-off family it would seem in Pakistan and lived in Maida Vale – a district somewhat more upmarket than Barbara's. And so began our courtship. It was not love at first sight, but I was smitten, and I think, being so far from home, eager to have someone to take care of me. We would go to the cinema, for walks in London's many parks, out for the occasional curry but, more often than not, he would call round to my flat, and we would go through coursework together, comparing notes and discussing exercises.

At some point during those long evenings working out formulae or doing complicated maths calculations, we would find ourselves kissing and cuddling and exploring one another. Qasim, as he was generally known, was younger than me and sexually inexperienced. For my part the only knowledge I had of the male anatomy was from the pages of my zoology textbooks! But with time one thing led to another, and before I knew it, I was starting to feel changes in my body, getting very tired and zoning out in lectures. And when my monthlies stopped, I knew. I couldn't ignore it any longer: I was pregnant!

I am not sure which was harder: telling Qasim or writing to inform my mother in Guyana. Her daughter Olga, who had left home to such fanfare and with great ambitions, pregnant and unmarried! Of course, my mother's response was one of anger and disappointment, but to be fair to Mohammed, his reaction was that, despite our youth and cultural and social differences, the only thing – the right thing – to do was to get married. However, we didn't quite do things in the correct order as our son Mohammed Sabir was born on January 2, 1961 at a hospital near Paddington and we did not marry until August of that year, at the registry office in Harrow & Wealdstone.

Despite the wrath of my mother and the imposed

hiatus it meant for my studies, I was delighted to be a mother. For Qasim though, things were a little more complicated. His parents had never met their new daughter-in-law, I wasn't a Muslim, and I was from a different social class from their son. Moreover, it transpired that Qasim had been betrothed from birth to a cousin in Pakistan – something he singularly failed to mention to me at any point earlier in our relationship! His parents responded by cutting off his financial support.

Reality struck. By then we were all three living in his flat in Elgin Mansions in Maida Vale's Elgin Avenue, which was not cheap. There was nothing for it but to get out and work to make ends meet. Our studies were shelved indefinitely. Qasim started working for the Gas Board while I, once I had arranged childcare (a lovely lady who went by the name of Sheila), took up a post at Abbey National. We settled into a routine of sorts and three years after our son was born, we had our daughter Salma.

There appeared to be a thawing in relations with his parents because we then started talking about moving to Pakistan. These plans began to gain momentum to the point where we even shipped some of our belongings out there, including some of the children's toys. I was, however, secretly terrified by the prospect of moving to a strange country even further away from Guyana, and to a very different culture. I was also starting to see a different side to Qasim: he certainly could be quite pompous and self-centred. My misgivings were fuelled further by my parents' own concerns that once in Pakistan I would have no control over my own children. Eventually I confessed to Qasim that I couldn't face going.

Undeterred, Qasim travelled to Pakistan ostensibly for a couple of weeks to see how the land lay with his family, but his return kept being delayed for various reasons. Weeks turned into months, and I began to realise he was probably not coming back. Though I can look back on that period quite calmly now, at the time I was distraught. I had grown to love Qasim, or so I thought; and I needed a partner to help support me and the children. Financially it would be a huge struggle to continue working and meet childcare costs. But I had no option. Somehow, I had to cope and carry on alone.

So, imagine my surprise, indeed shock, when several months later I happened across him in a shopping centre near Paddington! I couldn't believe that he had been back in the country and not come straight to see us, or his children at least.

"Olga, I am so sorry. Things have been difficult. My parents took my passport to stop me from coming back so I had to try and get another one. A friend of mine in the government managed to arrange it for me." He added that his parents had acquiesced on condition that he return to London and achieve his aim of going to university and that "he had meant to get in touch". All a bit implausible but I was prepared to clutch at straws.

Qasim moved back in with us and Salma at least was delighted to have her Daddy back We moved not long afterwards to a plusher flat in West Hampstead with a balcony and a bedroom each for the children. I was not sure how he was managing to afford the rent on such a property, but I assumed he had patched things up with his parents and they were once more supporting him financially.

We muddled along for a while but all the time I felt he was unsettled. He showed no signs of taking up his studies again. We argued more and more. He then announced he had to go to Pakistan as his mother had died. I can't remember how long he was away on that occasion but when he came back, it seemed she had had a miracle recovery. Maybe it was simply a ploy by his father to get him back to Pakistan, but by then I had little faith in anything Qasim told me. When he left for the third and final time, I knew it was over. It was hard but there was a part of me that secretly sighed with relief. Now I knew where I stood and at least I was facing the future in a country I knew and loved, and not all alone in Pakistan. Of course, the children were distressed, though each reacted in his own way. Salma took it out on me in fits of anger: she had loved her Daddy, and he had abandoned them. Mohammed Sabir, by now of school age, responded by changing his name to Simon, by which he is known to this day. I had to hold it together for the children most of the time, but once they were in bed and asleep my emotions would get the better of me. I would veer between tears and anger, and on one occasion resorted to tearing up all the photos I had of him. Only one survives but I have torn off the part with my image.

We never heard from him again – at least not directly. His brother wrote to me apologising for Qasim's behaviour. By all accounts he returned to Pakistan and was reconciled with this father, and duly and dutifully married his cousin. His parents apparently didn't even know he had married in London and had two children! I am not clear if he wedded his cousin before he was officially divorced from me, but I do know that the marriage to his cousin – despite the lengthy bethrothal and the hopes of his parents – did not last. I was left to pick up the pieces and arrange the divorce proceedings at Wood Green Courts.

And thus ended that chapter of my life.

Mohammed Qasim.
The only photo I kept of my husband
(the white smudges on the right are where I
tore off my side of portrait!).

My Husband

He's handsome, yes I know that!
He's clever... well, let's have a chat...
... Clever at thinking he's never wrong,
... Clever at choosing the very last song.
... Clever at picking the time to react,
... Clever at making my moods so abstract!

We have a love that we both feel,
A relationship just as strong as steel.
Without that I could not understand
Or maybe would make some type of demand.
To check him before he starts to tease
And make him understand just how to please.

But I don't need that, our love's too strong!
However, I ~~know~~
~ When I am RIGHT ~
~ and he is WRONG!! ~

My Husband: A little bit of exasperation with Qasim starting to creep in here, I detect.

8
And Then We Were Three

I DECIDED IT was time to take stock of my life and move forward. I had come to the UK to study at university and began looking at ways and means of achieving this. For a period, I had to keep working full time, moving in due course from the Abbey National to the Gas Board and eventually to Granada Television Network where I worked as an auditor. I was determined not to depend on others, and my mantra of the day was "I will never claim the dole." I also stubbornly refused to buy anything on tick or hire purchase and so had to scrimp and save for quite some time to be able to afford things – a washing machine for instance.

To make ends meet we moved to a flat in Rodbourne Avenue in North Finchley where I was lucky enough to come across a lovely Irish neighbour Peggy who became my trusted childminder. Armed now with the required new A Levels, I applied to do a Bachelor of Education degree with Science and Maths at the College of All Saints. The college, an affiliate of the University of London, was located not too far from North Finchley in Tottenham's White Hart Lane and I was able to take young Salma, who was still under school age, to the college's creche during the day.

Despite the pressure of being a mother and full-time student, I loved my three years at college. I had a generous study and maintenance grant and long holidays to spend with Simon and Salma. Most importantly, I was inching towards my lifelong ambition of becoming a teacher. I finally graduated in 1973 and while my mother had had hopes of my becoming a doctor, she was nevertheless proud when I received my BEd title. After all, her eldest brother, my Uncle Gladstone, had been a teacher and eventually a headteacher, and one of his daughters followed him into the teaching profession. And in fact, given the opportunity, I am sure my maternal grandmother Mathilda, the one from Barbados, would have become a teacher. She was born to it: she had a way of sitting you down and explaining things so clearly – and often in poetry form!

My graduation took place in the sumptuous and historical setting of the Albert Hall opposite Hyde Park, and my degree certificate was handed to me by none other than Queen Elizabeth the Queen Mother! I can imagine I shot up even further on my mother's pride scale when I wrote and told her this. After the ceremony itself we headed off to a reception at Westminster Abbey though somewhere along the way my mortarboard blew off and had to be retrieved from under a parked car much to the amusement of my friend Sonja and myself.

*

My graduation. Finally achieving my degree – and from Queen Elizabeth the Queen Mother no less!

It didn't take me long to find a teaching post. As a student I had experienced teaching practice in both primary and secondary schools, and while my maths and science training would have been put to good use teaching O Levels in those subjects, I was intimidated by some of the bigger, older boys who often arrived late, put their feet up on the desk and chewed gum all the way through class. I felt I would thrive more in a primary school environment and was delighted, therefore, to land myself a job at Northside Primary in North Finchley. Also, I could call upon my earlier A Level studies from Guyana to bring the children on in English grammar, comprehension and spelling.

And that was where I stayed throughout my formal teaching career. My first class was what today would be a Year 4 group – 8 to 9 year-olds. I loved the work and the children although I did encounter some hostility from one of the mothers who, it would seem, had taken a dislike to the colour of my skin (remember this was still 1970's Britain). She was generally quite unpleasant and addressed me off-handedly as "Mrs Whatever-your-name-is".

Again, the three of us, Simon, Salma and myself, settled into the new routine of school and teaching. Far from my family, effectively a single mother with two young children, I had no option but to keep myself busy and my emotions at bay. I had always enjoyed writing but now I threw myself into it as a sort of therapy: poems – mainly autobiographical ones – and stories for the children just poured out of me at this time.

The children preferred my bedtime tales to many of those in their story books. There was the one about the old woman who went on all sort of adventures, the dog who did funny things, another about a set of twins. Some of these tales were just *ad hoc* off the top of my head at bedtime; others, like "My Double Lives in Space" made it onto paper in booklet form, often illustrated by the children themselves. A few of these rudimentary stories eventually even entertained my pupils at reading time and – hopefully – inspired their imaginations

Around this time, my half-brother Eric came to live in London. Uncle Eric was a great favourite with Salma and Simon: in particular, it was Uncle Eric who took Simon to football practice on Saturdays, yours truly having little interest in the game and usually too busy writing or studying to have time.

Eric eventually married and moved to south London. On a trip to Paris, his two children were tragically killed in a motor accident, contributing perhaps to his subsequent parting of the ways from his wife. Eric returned to Guyana and toyed with the idea of buying some land and building a house. Gradually we lost contact, so I don't know if he realised his ambition, either in Guyana or Trinidad, which is where I believe he ended up.

Then younger brother Ken came across to the UK. As children we had been very close: at one year younger he was the nearest in age to me. We had our moments though: I can remember us fighting one day over who could hold baby brother Maxie and in the heat of the moment we ended up dropping him (with no lasting damage I hasten to report!).

Although Ken's plan was, like my own, to study in the UK, this never amounted to much and he eventually ended up working in a local government office. I was delighted having him close at hand in London, and he spent a lot of his free time entertaining Simon and Salma who simply adored their young uncle.

It was useful having him around at the time as Olga Qasim, never one to simply tread water, decided it would be an interesting thing to do a master's degree! Simon was about ten and Salma five when I enrolled on an MSc in Entomology – the study of insects of all things – at Birkbeck College. This London school specialises in part-time and evening courses for working people, so I was able to carry on teaching during the day. It certainly didn't leave me much time for socialising or anything else.

Ken was a godsend, but the gods weren't quite so very kind to him. He contracted glandular fever while he was in London and with his health already compromised by an earlier bout of pneumonia, was unable to withstand the effects of the virus. He died in 1968 in his early 30s and I mourned him dearly.

9
Olga Qasim: Teacher - And Houseowner!

AS I GRADUALLY made my way up the career ladder from probationer to more senior posts, and as the children got bigger, my thoughts turned towards somewhere more spacious to live. The Rodbourne Avenue flat had served us well, but Simon and Salma really needed separate bedrooms by now, so when a new council housing development opened up below High Barnet, I leapt at the chance to move into one of the flats there. It was brand new, a maisonette on two floors giving us so much more space. As a single mother I was entitled to a reduced rent, so it was actually cheaper than our old privately-rented flat. It was just a bus ride for Salma and me to our school and also for Simon who by now had graduated to the boys' secondary school in Finchley.

Money was still tight, though, and quite often I would walk home along the High Road from North Finchley to High Barnet to save on the bus fare. I did not want to stay in rented property for the rest of my life so was trying to put some money aside each month in my deposit account at the Abbey National.

One day on my walk home I came across a small heist of banknotes – some £40 which was quite a lot of money back then – under a parked car. Honest Olga that I was (and hopefully still am), I gathered up the notes and took them to the nearest police station. When I tried to hand them in, however, the constable on the reception desk told me it would be impossible to trace and verify the owner and to take the money home with me: a case of finders, keepers. With the blessing of the law, therefore, I made my way home with a lightness of step and a full shopping bag of food. We ate well that night.

School and the children kept me pretty busy so my social life was limited. From time to time, I would have an evening out with my work colleagues but after my experience with Qasim I had no time nor appetite for another man in my life. My friends tried some attempts at match-making and I remember a certain gentleman named Val valiantly phoning me almost every day for quite a while until it became clear I was not in the market for romance.

That being said, it came as something of a challenge when, with both Simon and Salma in their teens, a new baby, Sarah, came into my life. I certainly had my hands full then with three children to look after and a full-time teaching job. But it did prompt my mother into coming to visit from Guyana for the first and indeed only time. It had been some years since I had seen her, and I was over the moon. The children too were cock-a-hoop to meet their grandmother. She stayed for several weeks, and I felt like I was leaving Guyana all over again when she departed.

We continued to muddle through. Simon and Salma were old enough to look after Sarah when I was kept at work or when I was doing extra tutoring in the evenings to help bolster our Abbey National nest-egg. I would also work at summer holiday camps and schools to earn extra pennies, taking the children with me for several weeks. For young people in the UK today, especially in London where property prices are so high, it might appear crazy that I, a working mother with no partner and three children to look after, should have aspired to *buy* a property but I did just that.

My friends Ann and Fred Jarvis steered me in the direction of the Teachers' Building Society. This institution was established in 1966 precisely to help young teachers secure a mortgage with low deposits and at accessible interest rates. These mortgages were available to single teachers, both men and very importantly women: remember, at that time in the 1960s women often still needed a man's permission to open a bank account! And so, after much scrimping and saving and hard work, in 1981 when Sarah was two, I signed on the dotted line and handed over the deposit for the house in Fernwood Crescent where I still live. £39,850 might not seem much in terms of today's property prices but to me it was a small fortune. Nevertheless, I was happy and secure: Olga Qasim: mother, teacher and homeowner!

10
And The Rest Is History.. And Poetry And...Peace

WE LOVED THE house in Fernwood Crescent from the outset, although with a mortgage and three youngsters to feed and clothe, money was always tight. But the children had more space and a garden to play in, and I was enjoying my job at Northside Primary enormously. I taught at different times both Year 4 and Year 6 groups and while there were challenges, I seemed to cope with them and was known as the teacher "who never had to shout".

The social mix at the school started to change. When I first began teaching, the demographic was almost entirely white but then in the late 1970s we saw a great influx of Indian Asians mainly fleeing persecution from Idi Amin in Uganda. Other non-white, non-British children added to this, many of whom knew little English so we would have to send them to a special language unit off site. We later started to see an increase in children with special educational needs – partly as the social mix changed but also as recognition and diagnosis of conditions such as dyslexia and autism improved. I was lucky in that I had an excellent SEN Teaching Assistant in Joyce who performed miracles with even the most boisterous or complex of pupils, bringing them on in their learning and sending them home calm and fulfilled.

As a natural progression in my teaching career, I did start looking at more senior posts as they came up. I never really wanted to be a full-time headteacher as I would have lost my much-cherished daily contact with the classroom, but I did at one point apply for the deputy headship which was becoming vacant. I was unsuccessful and an outside candidate was appointed instead – someone that in my eyes had less experience. It would be difficult to say for certain whether the colour of my skin played a part in this decision, but you just never knew in those days.

The curriculum was also undergoing changes, with ever more emphasis being placed on the academic subjects and achieving standardised targets. I complied as much as possible but took every opportunity to broaden the content of my classes and make them more interesting.

For all the teaching and tutoring I did professionally, it rarely extended to my own family: Sarah, in particular, baulked against my trying to coach her at home but she did consent to be helped by Simon. The three did however continue to enjoy my stories and poems and always avidly read the latest one. Unbeknown to me, Salma entered me for a poetry competition: not any old poetry competition but that of the International Society of Poets. Imagine my surprise when I was shortlisted and invited to their 1999 Convention & Symposium in Washington DC!

I was even more taken aback when I won first prize which, apart from the trophy I still have in my sitting room, entitled me to have a book of my poems *Observations and Reflections* printed at no cost. A published poet! I wish my Grandmother Whittaker had still been alive for me to send her a copy: after all she had been my muse those many years before. On a second occasion, in 2004, I was once more shortlisted for the competition, and this time came away with an Outstanding Achievement in Poetry award as well as a cash prize: very nice thank you.

Life was good: work was rewarding, and Simon, Salma and Sarah were happy and doing well at school. But whether it was the stress of my early years in the UK and marriage to Qasim, or the richness of my mother's home cooking back in Guyana, I started to notice some pain and pressure in my chest. When it had gone on too long for it to be merely indigestion, I yielded and went to see my doctor. Between the symptoms and family history – my father, who never smoked and barely drank, had died in his 70s of a heart attack – before I knew it, I was in University College Hospital in central London having triple heart by-pass surgery.

After a month or two to recover, I was back teaching my Year 4s and once more home tutoring. But even I had to admit that, now in my late 50s, I was finding it a bit too much. Teachers had a pretty good deal in those days: retirement beckoned and with it the prospect of a lump sum with which I could pay off the rest of my mortgage. And so I reluctantly said goodbye to my classroom and my colleagues at Northside, though it was to be many years before I completely removed myself from the school, continuing to provide reading assistance and help in other subjects on a part-time basis well into my 70s.

And thus my life in London has continued. Simon, Salma and Sarah are all now adults with their own lives, children and indeed grandchildren making me, Olga, a great-grandmother. Simon, who like his mother always loved reading, did not, like me, become a teacher but eventually found his way into the Civil Service. Salma took a degree in English and did follow her mother into the teaching profession, although she has always been very musical – a nod perhaps to her Guyanese great-grandfather's family. Sarah had a very wide variety of interests and hobbies growing up but, similar to myself, ended up studying for a Science Degree with Maths in Leeds and has spent much of her life as a systems analyst. They have each had their trials and tribulations but today, I trust, are happy and fulfilled – just as I feel. I couldn't be prouder of them.

Even as they moved up and out into homes of their own, the nest never seemed to remain empty for too long. Nephews, nieces and great nephews and nieces have come through the revolving doors of Maison Olga over the years, either to study in London or tour the UK and Europe. My brother Eustace's granddaughter Stacey lived with me when she came from the USA to do a PhD. Her cousin Kevin also came to study and made my house his base. Jean's youngest son visited with his family just last year. And so it continues.

My immediate family live close by and visit regularly. My circle of friends may have got a little smaller as the years go by though I still see some of my fellow teachers for lunch. Of my close friends Ann, sadly, is now in a care home but still knows me after all these years. My lifelong pal Sonja came to the UK as a young widow a few years after me, leaving her children at home in Guyana, until she completed her studies. After her second husband died and her children were older, she and I went on many happy holidays together, to Spain, France, Portugal and elsewhere, bound in friendship by our Guyanese roots, our mutual interests and enforced spirit of independence. Those happy days of holidaying are over for Sonja who lives nowadays with her daughter, but I cherish every memory.

Guyana seems a long, long time ago. I have been back several times but not for the past decade. The children visited too and loved meeting their family there. I doubt I will have another opportunity to return to my homeland – especially as most of my family is now here or in North America. But Guyana will always be there in my memories, photos, poems and occasionally, too, in my dreams. Guyana is what made me; Britain is what shaped me. I am Olga Qasim – but deep inside too I am that little girl Olga Armstrong marshalling the local children into Mum and Dad's sitting room in Vreed-en-Hoop for their summer holiday lessons.

Oh! There's the doorbell ringing. Time for my next tutoring session. Will I ever give up teaching? I doubt it.

* * *

different part of Wonderland. It was Storybook Meadow. They found themselves in the middle of the story they all knew well. It was the story of the Three Little Pigs and the Big Bad Wolf. Robert never did understand why all of the Pigs could not live in the same house so he suggested it to them. They had actually thought this was a brilliant idea and asked Robert to help. In fact, Charlotte and

An extract from Storybook Meadow, one of the many stories I penned to keep my own children – and indeed some of my school pupils – entertained.

Tropical Rain

The raindrops fall down on a tropical town,
Kissing the earth as they softly come down.
The blue skies weep silently with a determined will,
As the tall trees stand so obediently still.
Look at the raindrops, feel the power
They start with a drizzle then turn to a shower.
Touch the warm drops, see how they glisten,
What a lovely sound, just stop and listen

The raindrops make circles on the stagnant pool,
There are shrieks of delight as drenched children run to school.
Fishes continue to dart to and fro,
As the attack of the rain on their home starts to grow.
Watch the patterns the circles make,
Look how the waters quiver and shake.
Dodge the raindrops as they fall down,
On this delightful tropical town.

Large puddles are formed on the old cobbled streets,
The traffic swishes by in their fleets.
Ladies walking briskly, coloured umbrellas held up,
Topped with the glistening water from each raindrop.
Jump in a puddle, make a big splash,
Watch it fill up again in a flash.
Drink in the dazzling colours that go by
As the tops of umbrellas point to the sky.

Tropical Rain, probably composed on a cold, grey afternoon in London in the 1970s

The Split

The man I met and married once
Is now a total stranger.
We should have known the match was wrong,
Our love was in real danger.

We came from worlds too far apart,
We never should have wed,
Our parents warned us of the fate
They ultimately dread.

How young we were and foolish too,
We should have stayed good friends,
Words written in that fated book
Were 'Match begins, then ends'.

I look back and I think how odd,
I cannot place his face,
Yet we who really were so close
Pushed far apart as space.

The man I met so long ago,
Had made me wife and mother
But really due to his culture
He should have wed another.

I do regret, I must admit,
The suffering and the pain.
But I expect, given the chance,
I'd do it all again.

Facing life as a single mother, poetry was a sort of therapy for me

Don't Give Up Guyana

Don't give up Guyana for your children's sake,
Look to the future, let your rich earth awake!
You're blessed with sunshine all the year round
And the many rich soils which can be found

Scatter your seeds a-plenty, let them flourish and grow,
Land of Many Waters, let your silver rivers flow.
You hold all the powers to decide your fate
You store up the riches so open up your gate!

Don't give up Guyana, lift your eyes to the sky,
Hang on to your beauty, you can if you try.
Your brown earth holds such riches as diamond and gold,
If you work together, they will ultimately unfold.

Don't give up Guyana, your future is bright,
Release your birds of wisdom, let your hopes take flight.
Teach your children qualities their ancestors had,
They had all the wisdom to make good from bad.

Don't give up Guyana, take your rightful place,
You can be a winner in any race.
Don't give up Guyana, you're still very great,
Keep your prospects growing, don't just sit and wait!

Trusting that my compatriots back in Guyana would continue to cherish the country that I remembered

No Time To Say Good-Bye

Suddenly he wasn't there,
My dearest younger brother.
He left this world and those who care,
To find rest in another.

It's strange to think though we were close
I had no sign or warning,
His parting words were never said,
I hoped he was returning.

I think of him 'most every day
He has left such a gap,
He went in just the strangest way
He didn't say good-bye.

I fell I'm left a-limbo,
That maybe I imagined
I saw his smiling face somewhere
But somehow can't remember.

The message came to me one day
by phone - an unknown voice.
"Your brother has just passed away"
No words could part my lips.

I cannot bear to visit,
His cold home underground,
I'd rather think that he's still here,
He's lost and will be found.

Death, how you swiftly steal away
Those whom we love and cherish,
No one escapes your stony clutch
Which leaves just memories.

So many words were left unsaid,
So many tasks unfinished,
With mission so unaccomplished
He's rushed off in a hurry.

You pass this earthly way but once,
So hope you've done your best,
When time's cut short you cannot tell,
If you have passed the test.

No parting words nor kiss on cheek,
He whould have, if he could,
His sudden illness left him with
No time to say good-bye.

I was very close to my brother Ken who was next in line to me. He spent some time in London hoping eventually to study, but illness took him at an early age, and I missed him so much.

Caught Up In The H.P. Trap

Just take a stroll down any High Street,
The signs are there to see.
No deposits.. Step right here
You've got three years to pay.

You go in, just to take a look.
Someone stops you on the way,
"T.V? Dishwasher? Washing machine?
Buy now, three years to pay."

You stop and think, 'Why ever not!'
The tele's on the blink
Your hands are raw from washing up
And you have three years to pay.

"Come sit here on this comfy chair
And fill up all these forms.
Sign here, No there, just by the X.
That's it, three years to pay.

We'll get them to your house real soon,
You go home and you wait.
You sit and watch the special gaps
To fit the goods you've brought.

The doorbell goes, you race to it
"Hello dear, we've brought your stuff".
"Please put them here and thanks to you,
I've got three years to pay."

The payment date has now arrived,
You send off your remittance
Three years don't seem that long to you,
But with interest your debt grows.

No one explained how H.P. works
Payments go on and on,
So before the end you find that you
Will have to start again.

Back to the High Street shop you go,
To make the self same purchase
You thought they'd last more years than three,
How wrong you were, for certain.

~ ~ ~ ~

When the children were small money was always tight, but I was determined never to live beyond my means.

My Home land

A distant voice keeps calling me
From somewhere in the past.
You left those shores so long ago,
You must return at last.

That voice it floated from afar,
Just carried by the wind.
My home land beckons, I must go
I've been away too long.

I joined a queue of hopeful souls
Just craving some adventure.
It was some thirty years ago,
The month it was September.

The land I knew so plush and green
Is foreign in my heart
It holds the secret of my birth,
Yet returning means a fresh start.

A hand extends across continents,
Just tugging at my soul
Please take this trip down memory lane,
And fill the gap you left.

But memories fade with passing time
That's what we seem to think
Can time really erase the past?
Taking one's own identity?

The giant magnet pulls me back
To the core of my homeland
The repellent nature on rebound
Loads up uncertainties.

The doubts I feel are quite natural,
The fears are that I'd find
The place I one time occupied,
Has long ago been filled.

My homeland calls, I cannot go.
I cannot face the changes.
I'd rather keep the imagery
Of things I left behind.

~   ~   ~   ~

Penned on one of those nostalgic days where I felt torn between the Guyana of my birth and my adopted home in the UK.

www.ingramcontent.com/pod-product-compliance
Lightning Source LLC
LaVergne TN
LVHW010317070426
835507LV00026B/3436